WINGS TO YOUR THOUGHTS

PUBLISHED BY WORDS OF SOUL

RAHUL B R

ISBN 979-888530221-0

Contents

Contents

Contents

Preface

This book express the thoughts and feelings of each and every writer. Each and every writer has expressed themselves differently and very beautifully. The book upholds the beauty of thoughts and shows it has no limit, many people said there is some limit to everything like sky is the limit, few length or distance is the limit and much more but, no one ever said thought has a limit because it has no limit at all, the more you think the more you get new thoughts to write.

This book is published under "WORDS OF SOUL PUBLICATION" and complied by Rahul.B.R. Here 30 co-authors have amazingly laid down their work on the topic "WINGS TO YOUR THOUGHTS"

Acknowledgements

First of all, we bow before the revered God Shiva. Due to whose grace our work was completed smoothly. Heartfelt thanks to the team of Words of Soul Publications and for their support. I express my heartfelt gratitude to the family members and to all the writers without whom this book would have been impossible. They gave their valuable time and cooperation as well as kept their faith in us and played their incomparable and unbelievable role in the completion of this book and once again thank you all from the bottom of my heart.

Thank you

Dr. Nikita Dudagi
Antara Choudhury
Akash Chaurasiya

Rahul B R

Compiler

He is Rahul.B.R
He was born in 19/09/1999 Ramanagara district, Karnataka.
But he is perceiving his higher studies in Bangalore. He has
completed bachelor degree in science. He like to know more about
literature and want to study more and more about it...
He started writing poems from past four years and he writes all
kinds of poems... on life, about nature's beauty, love and much
more. He is coauthored in many books, Compiler of the book called

"The Song Of Nature" and "Nemophilist" and also his poems has been published in his college magazine too.

MY PROMISE

I promise to love you
Even when you are bad
I promise to love you
Even when you got failed

I promise to love you
Even when you are ugly
I promise to love you
Even even you are dead

I promise to love you
Even when you are married
I promise to love you
Even when you have nothing

2

Shubhanjali Nishad

Name of Co Author is shubhanjali nishad she hailing from kanpur up. Her passion is writing. ND her hobbies is reading books ND travelling her aim is to achieve success in short time. She want to become a professional writer in his life.she completed 200+ anthology books as a co author contact with her through Gmail I'd
nishadrock96@gmail.com
Insta I'd kanha_ki_laado

प्यार और एहसास

तुम्हारे संग में रहना चाहता हूँ

मैं तुम्हें चूमना नहीं सिर्फ तुम्हें

देखना चाहता हूँ मैं तुम्हारी

यादों में रहना चाहता हूँ मैं

ना की तुम्हारी घनी जुल्फों

से खेलना चाहता हूँ मैं हरपल

मैं तुम्हें सबसे छुपा के रखना

चाहता हूँ मैं ना की तुम्हारे

होने का फायदा उठाना

चाहता हूँ मैं तुम्हारे बारे

में अपने घर वालों को

बताना चाहता हूँ मैं ना

कि तुम्हें भगा के तुम्हारे

दामन में दाग लगाना चाहता

हूँ मैं तुमसे बहुत प्यार करता

हूँ मैं इसलिये हमेशा तुम्हारी

इज्जत की लाज रखता हूं मैं

3
अनिता रोहलन

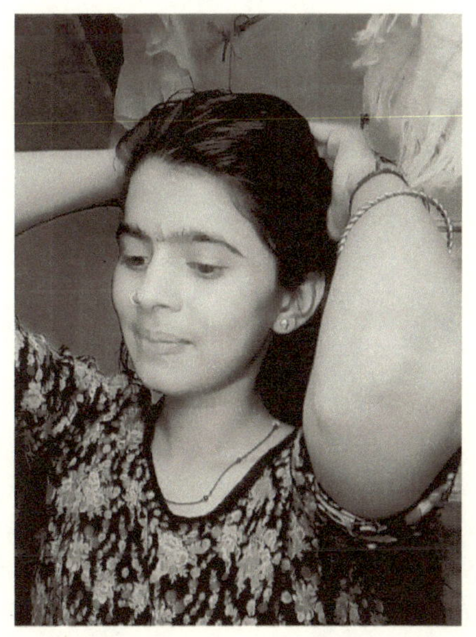

अनिता रोहलन (आराध्यापरी) का जन्म नागौर के जिले लाछड़ी गाँव में हुआ, इन्होनें बी.ए की पढ़ाई श्रीमती मोहरी देवी तापड़िया कन्या महाविद्यालय जसवनतगढ, लाड़नूँ से की, इन्हें खेल में भी रूचि हैं इन्होनें कराटे में रेड बेल्ट व ताईकावानडो यलो बेल्ट प्राप्त किया है इन्हें गानो के बोल लिखिना भी बेहद पसन्द

है। इन्हें नृत्य व योगा में भी बेहद रूचि है। यह प्रकृति प्रेमी है। इन्हें लिखना बेहद पसन्द है। पर यह इसे सामाजिक बदलाव का सशक्त माध्यम मानती है। इनकी 60 पुस्तकों में कविताएं प्रकाशित हो चुकी है।

है। इन्हें नृत्य व योगा में भी बेहद रूचि है। यह प्रकृति प्रेमी है। इन्हें लिखना बेहद पसन्द है। पर यह इसे सामाजिक बदलाव का सशक्त माध्यम मानती है। इनकी 60 पुस्तकों में कविताएं प्रकाशित हो चुकी है।

दुष्कर्म

न लाज न शर्म है

न कानून का प्रकोप है

यहां कानून को पूजा जाता है

फिर भी होते हैं यहां हर रोज बलात्कार

फिर भी हर सत्ताधारी मौन है

सर्वश्रेष्ठ देश है मेरा

हर मुद्द पर होते हैं बवाल यहां

फिर दुष्कर्म पर क्यो मौन है जग सारा

सीमा पर हमला करने वालो को

एक रात में उखाड़ फेका

चाहे कैसा भी कानून हो संसद बलि पास कर ही देती है

कोरोना जैसी महामारी के लिए वैक्सीन ले आये

फिर यह दुष्कर्म जैसी बमिारी का इलाज क्यो नही कर रहा कोई।

हर बार करते हैं वो किसी की जिदगी के साथ खिलवाड़

अब नही करगे का हवाला देकर

तार_तार करता है वो हैवान उसकी अस्मिता को

बवाल यह नही है कि दुष्कर्म करने वाला अपराधी है

सवाल यह है इतनी घटिया हरकत के बाद भी

हर पार्टी,हर राजनैतिक दल मौन है

बड़े मूल्यो,आदर्शो की गाथाये गाते हो ना तुम

तुम्हारा वो लाड़ला एक मिनट मे इस संस्कृति को शर्मसार कर देता है

आखिरि क्यो?

4
Shilpi Singh Rajawat

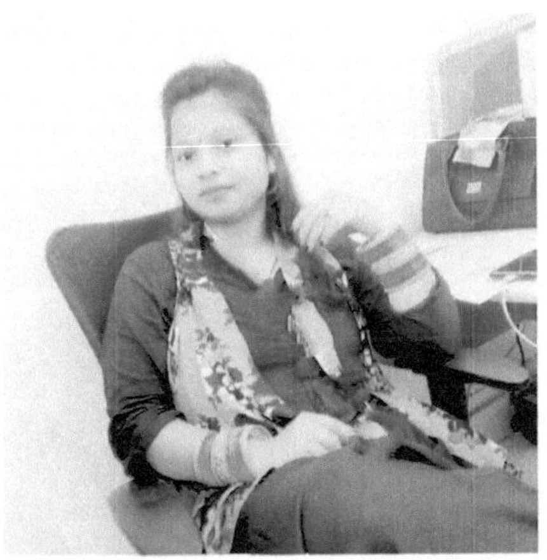

She is daughter of Shri Sangam Singh and Smt. Saroj Singh.She has completed her Graduation (B.A from Delhi University) and pursuing M.A in English from IGNOU. Her age is 24. She is from India (Delhi). She is a teacher and love reading to children. She belongs to middle class family. She is connected to maximum 250 Anthologies in part as co-author and participating in many writing communities.

She likes to write poetries, articles,short stories and motivational stories. She express emotions-feelings by her writing. She encourage herself and stand for women who are facing domestic violence. She want to do something women empowerment. She is a goal oriented person

शब्दों की उड़ान

बेसब्र हैं मेरे अल्फ़ाज़,

पन्नों में उतरने को,

दिल की धड़कन बता रही

अल्फ़ाज़ों की उत्सुकता को !!

मैं न रोक पायी इस उभरते शोर,

शोरगुल मंजर को,

अब उतर जाने दो इन्हें पन्नों पर,

दिल में भरे जज़्बातों को !!

क्या कहा साथ निभाओगे,

भूल न जाना इन बातों को

दुनिया की चकाचौंध में अक्सर

लोग भूल जाते मीठी मुलाकातों को !!

ख़ैर हमें तो आदत है,

लिखना और जख़्मी दिल की आवाज़ सुन

कागज़ में कलम के ज़रिये शब्दों का बखान

यही से मिली मुझे- मेरे शब्दों को उड़ान

5
Sanju Agarwal

He is Sanju Agarwal. He lives in Bihar. He completed his studies. He loves to write story, poem and Shayari.

दखेा जब उसे

दखेा जब उसे ...
दलि में आग लग गयी ....
वक्त थम गया
और धडकन रुक गयी ...
पास जाकर दखेा
तो चांद सी खलि गयी ...
कुरता जॅकेट में
अप्सरा सी मलि गयी ....
क़ातलि नगिाहों में
चमक उठी थी ...
उसकी हर मुसुक्राहट पे
सांसें रुकी थी ...
उसकी हर अदाओं पे
हम फदिा हो गए ...
जन्नत सी दखि गयी
और हम वफा हो गए ....

6
NOOR TABASSUM

The name of the author is Noor Tabassum. Writing is her passion. She has participated in more than 300 anthologies as co author and has also written solo books called Sensibles and Twisted Firsts. She is a nature lover and loves to lead a simple life. She expresses all her feelings in her writings as she thinks it is the most powerful medium to communicate. She has won many writing competitions, and her articles have been published in many magazines too. She enjoys writing poems and short stories. Her stories have been published in the Times of India newspaper too. Her Instagram id is @noortabassumali123.

SPREE

Every day brings with it new challenges and tests,

The most extraordinary task is to face it with a smile, and deeming it as a must,

After facing all these chores, life becomes dull, and without interest,

It craves for something unique to bring back the curiosity and makes us peacefully rest.

Small surprises bring unknown astonishments to life,

It may be devoting some time in a garden viewing stunning lives,

Or listening to music and going on an adrift drive,

Or observing the sunset or sunrise and experiencing paradise.

Have you ever observed the butterfly sloppily flying in a spree,

No one to stop it flying from flower to flower, completely free,

One feels so delighted and heavenly to see,

This passionate piece of joy, flying from tree to tree.

My heart hovers with it and relishes its spree,

I forget this world and want to distress it becoming a bee,

It would be prodigious amusement, I guarantee,

When cheery butterflies, fragile, aromatic flowers, and my heart
fly like a bee.

NOOR TABASSUM

IG ID - @noortabassumali123

7
Kaushiki Sarkar

Kaushiki Sarkar is an earthling since 11th May, 2004. She was born in Kolkata, India. In the year 2021 she had given her paintings in the exhibition for the first time and won an award for the best painter in still life painting category. She has also won many gold medals in painting.

She is Nyctophiliac.

She buried her thoughts and emotions inside her until she started writing. In the year 2020, she started writing. Writing is her antidote and passion.

She was featured in Taare Zameen Par Magazine. She has won the title of Miss. Spotlight 2021 by Ambitious Awards, Ace Of Initiative awards, Global Iconic Women Awards, Shahanshah Got Talent Award and Sparkling Scribbler Of The Year 2021.
She is the Founder of Inksteady Creative Community and Crystal World Community. She works with different writing communities as a graphic designer and community head.
She is a part of international magazines and worked in many world record anthologies.
Instagram I'd - @__tok_jhal_misti__

Lattern of My Life

You were like a lantern

That glowed the brightest,

During the darkest days of my life.

You showed me the path,

Held my hand with love,

And walked with me

Through the darkness to light.

You shined the brightest

Among the stars,

And gave me the courage to

Glow my inner light

And spread my wings.

Your light nourished the

Lifeless flower within me,

And helped me to bloom again.

8

Kavita Vijaywargiya

कवति वजियवर्गीय एक ४० साल की युवती हैं जो मध्यप्रदेश के गुना से संबंध रखती हों उन्हें संगिगि करना , लखिना , पढ़ना , बच्चों के साथ मस्ती करना ये सब बेहद पसंद हों धर्म से जड़ी हर चीज , हर बात उन्हें आकर्षति करती हों

.ख़त

माँ,

क्यों नहीं लिखा तूने मुझे ख़त

क्यूं रहती है अब लाचार इतनी

क्यों बना रही ख़ुद को बेबस

घर से विदा हुई हूं दुनिया से नहीं

बाट सके तू अपना ग़म

क्या ?

रही तेरी अब इतनी भी नहीं

मैं तो तेरा अंश हूं और तू जननी मेरी

तेरे ही रक्त से बनी थी ना

ये नन्ही सी गुड़िया तेरी

पढ़ने था जब मुझको भेजा

तब तो आता था ख़त तेरा

अब तो मैं इसी शहर में हूं

घर दूजा सही मगर तेरी नज़र में हूं

इतना भी मुझे पराया न कर

कि आ भी न सकूं मैं अपने ही घर

9

Kanish Ravinth J

The above poem belongs to kanish Ravinth J.18years old.I'm a student from JEPPIAAR INSTITUTE OF TECHNOLOGY.My hobbies are writing,reading, outdoor and indoor games.

Poetry !!!

The pen sat in the middle of

My fingers,

The top of my lap paper Crawl,

Travel the world of my thoughts,

Get the glory of my

Mother tongue,

Suppress comment within short lines,

To the amazement of

Those who read it,

To continue the tiers,

Poetry is the embodiment of this !

10

Mansi Rath

Mansi Rath is a young writer/poetess in English and Hindi. She hails from the heart of India – Raipur, Chhattisgarh. She is pursuing her masters in zoology. She has adored shayaris and nazams for ages which influenced her to become a Romantic poet. Her other interests are sketching, painting and capturing life moments. She aspires to become a novelist.

Truth

Tell me a truth

You never loved me ,

I'll tell you a lie

I never loved you.

Tell me a truth

You never cared for me ,

I'll tell you a lie

I never cared for you.

Tell me a truth

It never hurts you

I'll tell you a lie

It still doesn't hurt me

11
Kamini Pradhan

कामिनी प्रधान , जो ग्राम पोस्ट आमगांव, शाखा – तमनार , जिला – रायगढ़ छत्तीसगढ़ में निवास करती हैं , जो अभी एम.एस. सी रसायन शास्त्र में अध्ययनरत हैं , जो पढ़ने, लिखने के साथ साथ संगीत में रुचि रखती हैं ।।

"मायूस मन "

बहुत याद आती है आजकल तुम्हारी , दिल में दर्द होता है तुम बिन

बात नही होती तो लगता है फूलो की खुशबू कही खो सी गई है ....

तुम बिन न जाने आसमान तारो से भरे होने के बावजूद सुना लगता है ,

कहा को गए हो.. एक इशारा तो कर दो .....

कमि मैं भी कही तुममे ही गुम रहता हू, तुम्हारे इंतजार में रुका रहता हू,

कुछ टाइम की खुशी पर अकेलापन भारी पड़ जाता है यारा !

बात करने को तुमसे ये मन हमेशा करता है , मगर तुम भी न .....

एक मैसेज सेंड नही कर पाते और न ही बात पूरी कर पाते ....

डर सा लगने लगा है , उजालो की चमक में अंधेरे ने बसेरा कर लिया है ,

कभी अचानक से नजर के करीब तो आ जाओ ....

सालो हो गए देखे हुए तुम्हे , अब जिन्दगी क्या मोड़ लेगी पता नही ....

सब कुछ छूट नए जाए हमसे जरा बात पूरी तो कर लो ...

क्यू खामोश से रहते हो ...दर्द में जीने को क्यू तलाशते हो ...

तुम्हारी इच्छा जो तुम्हे ठीक लगे ....

मगर मुझे तकलीफ ना पहुचाओ ....देखते है अपना प्यार आजमाते है ,

कितना सच्चा है ये दिल तुम्हें लिखी हुई ये पन्ने तुम्हारे दिल को छू जाती है या नहीं

...

एक बार दिल से बात कर लो तुम ...

समझ जायेंगे हैं कुछ हमारे लिए तुम्हारे अंदर ...!!

12

Har Deepansh Bahadur Sinha

He is Har Deepansh Bahadur Sinha .
He belongs to Lucknow,UP.

He is a research scholar of Oceanography and has done masters in Geography from National Post Graduate College.
Completed his schooling from Study Hall.
His hobbies are art , listening to music , cooking & loads of driving. His interest areas are Astronomy,Writing,Photography & Travelling a lot.

Let's Empower to get Empowered

We must fight for women empowerment

For their happiness and betterment,

In any manner we should accept

Also we must give them respect.

We should raise them socially

Support them unconditionally,

Lets get serious about their education

Together we must save them from molestation.

Let them get independent psychologically

They will upgrade the society handsomely,

Women must empower themselves economically

To fight back any kind of tragedy.

One should also welcome them politically

Listen to their viewpoints sincerely,

Women are important to this world

Don't let their presence get whirled.

Women's should not be worried about criticism

They have the power to change the system,

So let them free and fly

Make sure they don't cry.

13

SANATKUMAR MISHRA

He is Sanat kumar Mishra a boy dwelling in the 15th year of his life & studying in Class-10. He is a writer and a pretty well artist. He was born and brought up in cuttack, odisha. He feels immensely pleasured to write poems about emotions & upheavals in life. He entered the arena of literature not long before 4 years when he wrote his first poem in English.

THE PLEASANT HEAVEN: MY GARDEN

Amidst all grievances of hectic life,

There lies a place of heaven, away of strifes!

This is a heavenly abode of mental solace;

That assimilates all sorrows within- to bring ecstasy.

O! Dear garden, you are the home of joys-

Who drives the dark clouds from life's toy.

You are the earth where glint of solace exists;

Making all afflictions of pensive life- vanish!

O! Dear garden, you are adorned with beautiful flowers-

Which are really blissful like rainbow showers.

The flowers glinting with diverse colours,

Adjust the emotions of the pained mind.

Those glorious flowers smile with happy faces-

Dresses up my profound wounds & traces.

The glee of flowers sings a lullaby-

Making me nostalgic of the bygone days.

Nostalgia growls over the isolated mind

& reminiscences over the childhood days- that rewinds!

The glare of the sun with the songs of theirs'

Throws aback the bleeding tears & welcomes peace.

Amongst the shinning blossoms, the buzz of bees-

Entangles the heart to jeer at the hiding devil with glee.

The gracious noise of tiny little insects-

Asks me, "are the dusky shadows really pensive?"

Then the flowers murmur with a boggle in their heart,

And the green glowing grasses shout like a smart!

Their whispers enriches the brain to answer-

"the dusk is pensive, but the dawn is ecstatic with you!"

The piety of the huge trees draped with sunshine:

Again flashes me back to the boyhood days- to whine!

I enjoyed the nostalgic memories of those days-

Resting on the carpet of grasses in my blissful garden.

The euphoric moments spent there jingles the inner core-

To lift the aspirations again & to march towards the shore!

The soil of the garden fertiles my swollen body;

Enhancing it to walk upon the thorns to the pinnacle!

"…. The pleasant garden astounds my emotions & fears;

But still recollects the picture of my dear:

Who was my best companion at all hurdles,

And my healing aid to all my hurts amidst the struggles!"

14
Manik Gupta

Manik Gupta. He is 23 years old. He is from Shamli(UP) and right now working in Gurgaon. He has suffered a lot in his life which has made him so much passionate about writing because this is the only way he can share his emotions with everyone. He

has worked as a co-author in more than 10 anthologies and looking
forward to more opportunities

My Heart

My heart stops beating,

My mind stops dreaming,

Feels like having someone,

Who can change my fortunes,

You are the only hope I live with,

My only trust,

Hope it remains always,

Hope you always remain you,

Hope my trust pay off on you,

Life would be nothing without you,

Every problem has a solution,

And my solution is just you,

May God shower his blessings on we both,

And never let that time come,

When I am there,

But without you.

15
Kripali Makhecha

Kripali is a student of life. She believes in always be a learner.
She is passionate about reading and writing since her childhood.

She likes to help people with their emotional and mental health issues.

16
Dreams were Myth

The baby is in danger" Doctor said and everyone in the family get panicked. They were speechless. Suddenly, one man with disappointment in his eyes spoke, " doctor please call the experts, do something.. on any cost just save my grandchild." The father of baby lost his conscious, tears were on his cheeks, his eyes were open but couldn't see anything.

The lady was pregnant after many efforts in upper middle class family. They all were exited and happy, even started planning for post delivery functions. There were just few days left for baby to see the new world and mother fell down from stairs. They were in hospital and all of their dreams started to become blur. Simple line between dreams and reality were clear in few minutes.

After a couple hours doctor came and said, " The new born baby girl is out of danger. We have to keep her in glass box for few days but there is no reason for worries" Grand father come to his knees, his wife joined hands to thank god, father of baby regained his consciousness; their dreams were becoming true and real once again. In a few minutes they started distributing sweets in whole hospital. Relatives were calling for congratulate the family, some were there for meet up. They started inviting people for baby born party.

Suddenly Doctor came again. His eyes were looking suspensions. Family was looking hopefully to doctor for some good

news. Doctor said with disappointment, " we're sorry, we couldn't save mother, due to heavy blood loss, she died."
They were planning to organise party and they didn't know they have to arrange funeral. All the happiness for few minutes were myth? Their dreams took turn to the some unknown route and everything just disappeared.

.

17
Himanshi Singh

This is Himanshi Singh, currently pursing B. SC from IT
COLLEGE, LKO. I believe that writing is my passion.

मंज़िल पाना आसान नहीं होता

मंज़िल पाना आसान नहीं होता

कठिनाइयां बढ़ती जाती हैं

अगर सिर्फ सपना देखा

मेहनत में एक जुनून होना होता है

तभी ना पाना भी मुमकिन हो जाता है

कुदरत भी हमें परखता है

कर्म तो हमें ही करना पड़ता है

फल और सब तो वही देता है

फिर भी मंज़िल पाना आसान नहीं होता ,

यकीन रखो दोस्त, यह खुदा है

देता तो है हमें हमारी मंज़िल, मगर उतना ही चलाता है यकीन पर तो दुनिया टिकी है

तो फिर हमें क्यों नहीं जलती है

मंज़िल पाना आसान नहीं होता

अभी मेरे सपने को उड़ान बाकी है

चले तो सिर्फ कुछ कदम ही थे, अभी तो पूरी रात बाकी है

कौन कहता है जनाब कि, ज़िंदगी किस्मत से चलती है वह तो हमारे कर्मों से बनती है

मंजिल पाना आसान नहीं होता

मंजिल पाना है, चाहे जितनी मेहनत करनी पड़े.

जिंदगी आसान बनानी है, चाहे दिन को रात बनानी पड़े.

योजना जितनी ही गुप्त हो, सफलता उतनी ही निश्चित है सघर्ष ही जीवन का मंत्र है, इसके बिना पूरा जीवन का अंत है

मंजिल पाना आसान नहीं होता।

18
Meera Gopalakrishnan

Meera Gopalakrishnan has been writing under the pen name Shruthi since 2018 when she first published her novel Seven Vows. She has also co authored 20 anthologies so far(15 in pen name Shruthi,5 as Meera). Before becoming a writer, she was working in IT industry and used to analyze TV shows like Diya aur Baati Hum, Ek Hasina Thi, Siya Ke Ram, Beyhadh etc. She loves Indian mythology, culture and Indian history and interested in weaving stories around that. She has an active profile in Wattpad shruthiravi13 and her insta id is mira_g_pai.

Symbol of Friendship

Gift the word itself takes me back to my college days. I studied in college when only the very rich among us used to have mobile and there were no ecards. We use to go to Archies ya Hallmark store to buy Birthday Card as gift for your friends. It was a time consuming process which we enjoyed. The cards were choosen carefully after reading each word. As the card represented how you viewed your friend. It was a representation of your relationship with your friend. Everyone waited eagerly for those simple birthday card gifts because we all wanted to know what we meant for our friends. I have to say I have got so many expensive gifts in my life. But nothing matched the happiness I got while reading those beautiful birthday cards gifted by my friends. Those were not just cards they carried the love and warmth of our friendship and the time people have invested in you as a friend.

19
Sannidhya Mishra

Sannidhya Mishra is a 16 year old girl from Odisha. She was never into writing but as she grew older she developed an interest in writing and wants to publish her solo book one day.

Being a guy

Being a guy is not easy

On you the whole family rely

They force you to earn

And you can't even deny

Being a guy is not easy

They always show you wrong

For a few people always

We are also blamed along

Being a guy is not easy

You have to be silent and rude

When there is a deep pain

All alone we stood

Being a guy is not easy

Tears are not allowed to come out

Your character has a stain forever

You are always in the arms of doubt

Being a guy is not easy

Your choices can't be different

They tease you with you lifestyle

They make fun of your accent

Being a guy is not easy

People think you don't have emotions

Just once try to understand us

There is hidden pain's oceans

20

Apeksha Khedkar

Apeksha Khedkar , a 14 years girl .
From Pune .
She writes Poems ,Shayari, Stories And Articles in 3 language
English ,Marathi and Hindi .

It feels her connected to herself as she explore herself every moment.
Inking her emotions and feelings is the best company of her life
.

Writing and Dancing is her passion

Travel!

Travel as you like,

Coz the world is large,

Larger than your life.

Coz the mountains are tall,

Taller than you all.

Coz the oceans are deep,

Deeper than your thoughts.

Coz the trees are big,

Bigger than your heart.

Coz the soil is strong,

Stronger than your might.

Coz the breeze is warm,

Warmer than your touch.

Coz the moon is calm,

Calmer than your sigh.

Coz the sun shine's bright,

Brighter than your smile.

And the pleasure thereupon is priceless,

Than the treasures you can buy.

Such is the place,

Where happiness you may find.

Written By – Apeksha Khedkar

21
Nithila Shri

in engineering. She's an optimistic person who cherishes music and books to be the best part of her life. The considers writing as

an opportunity to express her thoughts in simple words. This is her fifth anthology as a co-author. Besides being a co-author, she's also a singer. In her part of this anthology, she is sharing her real life experience with solitude and how it keeps her happy!
Instagram ID @_ambitious__queen_._

SOLITUDE

In this hectic world, I started falling in love with solitude. No! It doesn't make me feel lonely. Instead it always makes me feel comfortable with inner peace and happiness!

Yes darling! Many questions has aroused....

" Hey girl ! Don't you know how to mingle with people? " " You are weird and living such a boring life!" " If I live your life for one day, then I'll die for sure! " ..... These kind of words from others didn't stop me from loving my SOLITUDE!

Staying socialized is very important! But spending time with yourself is equally important. Solitude aided me in expanding my way of thinking, enhancing my creativity and bringing out the best in me! It has also taught me how to stay individualistic and has made me realise the reality of life!

None is permanent in our life except ourselves! So the utmost priority has to be given to ourself. No! I'm neither selfish nor egoistic. If I'm content , surely I'll be able keep to my surroundings happy. The reality is physical , social and mental health of every individual contribute to the wellness of this society and has a huge impact. Thus Solitude assists you in the betterment of your life. Being a co-author, solitude has helped me to expand my thoughts and knowledge.

Here's my final message.....

Live your life with immense pleasure and grateful heart. Always value yourself high. Stay grounded even if you reach great heights. Assign some time to spend with yourself and bring out your hidden talents.

" Cherish the solitude!

Build a good attitude!

Never fail to express gratitude!

You'll reach high altitude!"

22
Kashish Saxena

She is 19 years old, loves to write poems ans travel. Very fond of learning different cultures and languages. Loves to travel a lot and a big foodie. Likes to writes poems as hobby.

Old is Gold

Old is always be gold,

All of us talk about it,

Loving the songs of 90s,

Talking about the fashion during that time....

Let us see the change in clothes,

Let us see the transition of clothes,

From the Bell bottom to jeans with crop tops....

Now

1. Simple "Dupatta" converted into shrugs and tops too....

2. Simple light coloured dresses to embroidered, vary heavyweight dress or shimmer type dresses and etc...

Fashion has seen many changes,

Changes that brings new looks, new trends in every day,

Every cloth have it's fashion or defines it's beauty

Yes, true fashion brings its impact in every aspect of time...

Now let starts with the glance the transition of clothes...

• Starting with simple long or short kurtas,

To designers, printed, heavy ones for every occasion and up- down kurtas for daily uses...

• Simple Lehengas on weddings from branded or designers one's

• The Black and White Sarees on different occasions and changes into the transition like heavy materials works, heavy embroidered works or silk saree etc...

Fashion brings its looks in every persons with their personalities

23

Rampriya.P

This is Unicorn-RK,knowns as Rampriya.P, pursuing her
Ba.Political Science,2nd year,tamilnadu.
She is the daydreamer ,belives that dreams has powers too...

And gives her dreams the invisible golden wings to fly away
from this world!

24

Inside me unknown you!

On the morning sunlight
My legs slowly steps down my bed
My fingers searched the mirror
My first view is my face
Yeah! I love myself
My life crawls like this,
But on that day the boy crossed me
My heat beats fell in fire
My eyes becomes blind that his gaze
Get into me,
My legs becomes numb
Warmly love entered into my little heart slowly

25

ANNAPOORNI.E.G

Ms. Annapoorni is an undergraduate in English Language and Literature, and an avid writer hailing from Kerala. A student and writer by profession, but a human by passion, Annapoorni is currently a BEC Business Preliminary aspiring student from the Cambridge University, UK, who has also completed a crash course, as well as attended English Language training from the 'Orell' English Lab. She has so far co-authored nearly 75 Anthologies under various publications, and is compiling a book titled 'Life is Beautiful' under the Lost Pearl Publication, Orissa. Keen towards

Blogging, Proofreading, Content Writing and Translation, Tamil is her mother tongue, apart from which she is also eloquent in English, Hindi, Malayalam, and Sanskrit. Currently she owns a blog page titled "Blooming Thoughts" under the prestigious 'The Times of India' E-Readers Column. Historical Studies, Indian Writing, Political Science and Mythology are her areas of interest. She has published 3 articles for the reputed magazine The Namaste India E-Magazine, Pune, Maharashtra.

CORNUCOPIA

Was it necessary to leave us back?

She came to me like an angel with wings of colours and fire,

The shine that illuminated her body and soul with sparks of pain
somewhere,

Peeping through the window of my heart, she appears with a
chilling breeze,

That cools the soul and provides me warmth.

The fragrance of her sweat owing to hard work,

Fate dominating her life till the end

Never compromised but to attain salvation

Struggling alone in solitary.

Soon she leaves, leaving a piece of hope to survive,

Perhaps to exist rather with this peace and love for years and
years.

Angel she was, that stirred me a lot

To find her back, longing to stay in her warmth.

Abandoning her pillars, she bid us adieu, leaving behind a
Cornucopia for generations,

To learn, lead and love.

Craving for her erudite words each moment, I miss her pamper
and warnings,

As a teacher does, or a mom

With memories lying aside

In a heart filled with pain and passion.

I wish to fall for you again

Which soothes me like a peacock feather,

For your presence felt somewhere

Calls me back to lean onto your thoughts.

26
Ritu

Ritu from delhi
10th class student
I been co-author in many anthologies

कल जो हकीकत थी

कल जो हकीकत थी,वो आज बस एक सपना हो।

कभी रूठा करते थे जिससे बस लगता बस वही अपना हो।

बडी़ अतरंगी थी यारी अपनी।

लगती जान से प्यारी थी।

गुड़. सी मीठी,कभी खट्टी इमली जैसी थी।

साथ हुआ जो करते थे, आसमानों को हम छूते थे।

अब अलग अलग रहकर हम, जिंदगी जी लेते थे।

कभी हस्ते थे जोर जोर से,घंटो मिलकर बातो पे।

आज नही जब साथ वो पल, बस मुस्कुराते हैं ख्वाबों पर।

मिलना अब नहीं होता अपना।

ना जाने कैसी ये माया हो।

दिल घबराया था सोच के जिसको, दौर वही ये आया हो।

मिलना एक रोज होगा फिर से,सच्चे हम जो साथी हो।

वक्त भी लौटेगा एक रोज,जैसे लहरे लौट आती हो।

27
Emerald Reshma Reddithota

Student, Content Writer and Story Writer. Travel Lover.I have my works published at different platforms like Cityline Hitavada, a national daily newspaper, I have also my publications at my college magazine 'The Hislopian' which is a yearly magazine and also in a church magazine named 'The Cathedral Messenger' which is a bi-yearly magazine.

Dilemma

It's strange, it's very strange

That we live in the world

Which supports freedom of speech and expression,

But at the same time, it is the same world who suppress ideas,
especially younger ideas to satisfy the ego of so-called elderly,
powerful and adult people.

It's strange, it's very strange,

That we live in the world

Where we are encouraged to ask question or question things,

Where we are asked to keep track of everything,

But at the same time,

When we try to ask,

We are asked to shut up saying

'It's elders matter, don't interfere'..

It puts me in a dilemma

Should I ask or not?

Should I express myself or not?

28

Dr Major Nalini Janardhanan

Dr (Major) Nalini Janardhanan, is a doctor who served in Indian Army .She is a popular writer of Kerala who got Katha Award and a writer of many medical books for which she got IMA Sahithya Award. She is an Akashvani(All India Radio) and Doordarshan approved artist of Ghazals and Bhajans. She is felicitated with many awards

A DREAM

Dear Sumi,

How are you, my love? Sorry, I couldn't contact you for so long.

I want to share my dream with you in which I could feel us sharing the amazing emotion called 'love' even after so many years. We were in a hill station on a romantic trip. Dark shadows of trees were drawing beautiful designs on the lonely road. Hand in hand we were walking like teenagers enjoying the beauty of pine trees, blue hills, green mountain slopes, gushing streams and flower-strewn valleys. Forest and bushes were covering the mountains in a mantle of green looking like a carpet. Somewhere far away, a nightingale was singing a love song calling its lover. I remembered our favourite songs rekindling our love for each other...

The mist was covering the mountains like a white veil. There was a sweet fragrance of wildflowers in the wind. The time had come to a standstill and there were only the two of us in a different world of trance.

Sitting on the grass we enjoyed the beauty of the sunset. A sad song was coming from the valleys. I held you close to me, wiped your tears and requested you to smile. I told you that your dazzling smile was like a rainbow in the sky coming up when there is both sunlight and drizzling. Your smile comes straight from the heart and it takes my heart away.

Sumi, I miss you a lot darling.

-Your Anirudh."

-Dr Major Nalini Janardhanan

29
Shruti Dahikar

श्रुती दहकिर (जैन) महाराष्ट्र से हौ ये अपनी लेखनी से खुद को निखारना
चाहती हौ इस प्रकृती से बड़ा प्रेम हौ
अपनी सोच को, भावनाओ को खुद की कलम से अभिव्यक्त होने में ये रुची रखती
हौ

Insta ID- Shruti.heart_world

जतिना हैं हम...

मंजलि भलेही दूर हो,

रास्ते भलेही हमसे रूठ गये हो,

ख्वाईशो के पर भलेही कमजोर हो गये हो,

फिर भी जतिना हैं हम।

जिम्मेदारीयो का बोझा भलेही बढ गया हो,

ख्वाब कर्तव्य के तले भलेही दब गया हो,

हालातो की जंजिरि ने हमे भलेही जकड लिया हो,

फिर भी जतिना हैं हम।

जतिना तो हैं हम,

लेकिन अपनों को साथ लेते हुए।

मंजलि को पाना हैं हम,

लेकिन जिम्मेदारीयो को बखूबी निभाते हुए।

सपनो को साकार करना हैं हम,

लेकिन सबका दिल जितते हुए॥

-Shruti Dahikar ✍?

Insta ID-Shruti.heart_world

30
Sindhu Srinath

Sindhu Srinath has a Bachelor of Engineering degree in Electrical and Electronics Engineering as well as a Masters of Technology degree in Computer Applications in Industrial Drives and a Masters of Arts degree in Bharathanatyam. She has been awarded with Yuvashree and Saadhanashree from Mysuru Sanscrutika Pratishtaana. She co-wrote a book with G. Rashmi, Gaade Tili Bhaashe Kali - Learn Language through Proverbs which has been selected by CIIL (Central Institute of Indian Languages) for bulk distribution because of its use of incorporating both languages of English and Kannada. She has won intercollegiate poetry competitions and has published several poems and articles in Deccan Herald. She is also a trained classical singer, specializing in Carnatic Music. She loves reading and writing!

Fly

If only they could fly,

I would achieve so much.

If only they could fly,

They could be known to all.

For my thoughts are so many

And so diverse;

New ones arrive quicker

Than I could ever imagine

Or think!

If someone could give them wings

And let them fly and roam freely,

I could share them with others

And find like-minded people

Who would agree to my thoughts.

And make them reality!!!!

@Sindhu Srinath

Insta:- @reader75063

31
Sabrin Sultan

Assalamualaikum everyone! She is Sabrin Sultan presenting you a beautiful prose, feel it J..

YOU ARE MY DAWN OF TIME

When I sleep at night , Before that

I think of my siblings fighting?

But it never happened.. I smile J

And thought our relation.. is a mile.

Till dawn to dusk , I see brother and sister so playful

And I think of mine.. how silent we are.. but still beautiful.

The day starts with brothers and sisters.

Their playful and annoying moments , but taking care of each
other a lot !

This relation means a lot and it always does.

I know brother I know sister sun gonna rise in the dawn but,

Without you ... A day won't start...

The sun will diminish soon.. and the moon will take its place .. but
without you .. the day won't end..

I need you like a sun like a moon in my entire life!

With you ... you to start my day and end my day !

I know I dream of this everyday, But couldn't say.

But , seeing you the first makes my day

Seeing you last makes me stay.

Because, you are my dawn of time.

32
AASHIYA SUMAN

A poetess by passion and a shayara professionally,, AASHIYA
SUMAN is a personality who never ever believes in creating bonds,

lover of loneliness and a proud introvert, Writing is not just her hobby or something like it but her life

Uff vo Zid

जि़द करते हैं जब वो

करीब आने की,,,

मेरा लाख रोकना उन्हें

नाकाम.होता है!!

हुकूमत,,चलती है मेरे

रूह पर उनकी

ये जस्मि उनका

गुलाम.होता है!!

उस ,,बे- अदब.सी उनकी

महफ़लि में,,

हुस्न मेरा

नीलाम.होता है!!

मुझे छूते हैं जब

उन्हें रोक नहीं पाती

मुझ पर,,,,,हर मनचाहा उनका

काम.होता है!!

नज़रों से

मिलती हैं नज़रें

और,, लबों पर होंठों का

जाम होता हैं!!

फिर,, नज़ाकत से लिबास

हटती हैं तन से

उस,, बंद कमरे में सब

सरे-आम होता हैं!!

मुझे निशानी,, देते हैं वो अपनी

हर जरूरे पर

मेरे हर,, कतरे पर उनका

नाम होता हैं!!

हर छुअन उनकी

छू जाती हैं दिल को

पर,, दर्दनाक बहुत

अंजाम होता हैं!!

इश्क़,, करने का उनका

सलीका है ये,

इस बात से,मैं भी

वाकफ़ि हूं,

फरि भी उस ,,,

बेदर्द पर मेरा

बेदर्दी ,,का ही

इल्ज़ाम होता है!!

दर्द देती है उनकी,,

हर करीबयित मुझे

पर जो सच कहूं,,,,

उस,,,,,,

दर्द में एक

आराम होता है!!